Decorate *Fearlessly!*

Using WHIMSY,

Decorate CONFIDENCE,

and a Dash
of SURPRISE

Fearlessly!

to Create Deeply Personal Spaces

SUSANNA SALK

RIZZOLI
NEW YORK

New York · Paris · London · Milan

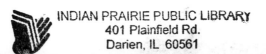

Contents

INTRODUCTION

A YOUNG DESIGNER ONCE ASKED ME, when it comes to selecting images for

my books, what special elements do I look for in a room? Her notebook

was open, she was ready to take notes. "More than certain characteristics,

it's more like indescribable feelings," I answered. "Like your heart is

engaged in a tango with

a delightful stranger;

like you have the sudden urge to pick up the phone and call your best

friend; like how the thought of leaving fills you with sadness, as though

a great novel is ending." There was a long pause as she just looked at me.

Esoteric emotions were clearly not going to cut it. "I suppose it comes

down to one of three words," I added and she immediately brightened:

"Wow. Huh! Yum."

After our conversation, I realized that some rooms often combine all

three words. It's these rooms I often refer to, over and over in my mind

When New Orleans artist Karina Gentinetta told me that she was sending
me one of her bold, graphic black-and-white paintings, my instinct was to hang
it in my entry hall. While her modern masterwork certainly merits a living
room placement, I love the surprise that its power brings to this cozy space and
how it completely enlivens the traditional sofa. It beckons and welcomes all who
arrive—including our rescue dog, Cheddar—and invites them to linger.

whenever I need help arranging my own home. Whether it's a living room in Provence or an entry hall in Boston, it's no matter. It's the spirit of the room that urges me to be more interesting with my own decor. It's not about copying, rather I take the bits that inspire me most—lamps with black lampshades, sheets with oversized monograms in chartreuse, five mirrors hung on a wall instead of one—and translate them into my own world with my own budget. I look to how they balance style and pluck as effortlessly as a French woman drapes her scarf around her neck and I forge on. After all, the rooms that play it too safe are always the ones you merely want to pass through, never linger in.

Whimsy had its very own chapter in my last book, *Be Your Own Decorator*, and I never tired of exploring its images again and again. Whimsy doesn't mean bragging about itself with showy pink kitchens, crazy sculptures dangling from the ceiling or bathrooms with waterfalls. Whimsical moments in rooms are the personal touches, the places where there is no fear, only confidence. Sometimes fanciful but always livable, whimsy expresses the owner's personality and always trumps any design trend. Whimsy holds the mood in a room in the same way that punctuation keeps a sentence both balanced and emotive.

I soon understood that every great room—no matter how grand or humble—exudes whimsy. It isn't simply a decor option, like choosing a fabric swatch or a paint color. Whimsy is a state of mind. But, to help people understand its importance I needed more of a mantra than an adjective . . . And then the rallying cry occurred to me: "decorate fearlessly."

Decorating fearlessly doesn't mean you have to be born a bungee jumper or sing show tunes in front of large crowds. You can acquire it, as I eventually have, just by seeing. Your design eye is a muscle: train it by exposing yourself to as many images as possible. Learn what you love, then embrace it. Remember that "supposed to" is one of the most dangerous phrases in all of decorating.

I hope that the decor in these pages will also cause you to say "Wow, Huh! or Yum." But I don't want you to simply admire and then turn the page. If something makes your heart dance a tango, you deserve to live with that delicious feeling every day. Whether painting your door a turquoise blue, covering your flea market chair in leopard, or hanging your grandmother's chandelier in your bathroom, go for bold both in little and big strokes. Once you begin, you'll realize it's the only way to truly express yourself.

In my own living room, I've used the fireplace mantel to display treasures of every origin to keep things lively both above and inside it. Faux topiaries bring green, no matter the season, and height, and a series of photographs my son took during our recent travels and gave me as a gift has been uniformly sized and framed to give a sense of a permanent collection. The bowls are from Target and are handy for keeping monogrammed boxes of matches inside. The screen is a luxurious hand-finished forged-iron pine bough scrim cast from antique architectural metalwork. It was like buying a necklace from Tiffany for the hearth. As long as the elements are well edited it can all cohabitate!

THE LIVING ROOM SPACE has been shortchanged as of late. Once the lynchpin of family life, the living room's status has been trumped by the increasing dominance of the kitchen or "family room," where eating mixes company with electronic screens, both large and small, and the art of conversation often takes a back seat to multitasking. So how to lure people

LIVING ROOMS

back into the space that once held much of the day's secrets and activities? By making it a player. Layer in enough of the practical and the whimsical, like Melissa Palazzo did in her Los Angeles family home on pages 18–19 with areas for lounging fireside that feel both groovy and cozy. Or, as in the case of James Andrew's Manhattan abode on page 21, you can infuse the space with so much chic color that it will, like wildflowers in a field, beckon all those who pass to spontaneously stop, gather, and linger.

Left: Jonathan Adler seamlessly intertwines formality and whimsy in this New York sitting room because every piece has design dignity. The pedigreed art allows the furniture—not to mention the flirty rug—to have fun that's never at the expense of the well-edited elegance.

Design by Jonathan Adler

Following Pages: "The inspiration for the room was a cozy, lush library," says designer Alex Papachristidis of creating his own exotic haven. "I wanted it to feel timeless, glamorous, rich, and opulent with yellow accents to pop. Be daring!"

Design by Alex Papachristidis

Right: "I love to mix periods and styles," says Lisa Sherry. "The modern lines of the fireplace update the home's 1920s-era architecture, but I also always try to be respectful of the provenance of the house, so the original mantel is hidden beneath. When designing boldly, it's good to keep options open in case the next homeowner chooses to unearth the original millwork."

Design by Lisa Sherry

Following Pages: "Adding a pop of an unexpected color is a great way to bring life into a space," says designer Melissa Warner Rothblum. Here, a living room she designed has a palette of mostly tonal blues, but by adding a kelly green settee in front of the fireplace, drama and excitement were invited in like eager yet elegant houseguests. "I love how unpredictable it feels!" she says.

Design by Melissa Warner Rothblum

Pages 18–19: "Doing the unexpected is fearless in my opinion," says designer Melissa Palazzo, who here applied her design mantra to her very own living room. "No matter the style, mixing different patterns, textures, and time periods are a must. In this room, a vintage wall covering mixed with contemporary art, some art deco furniture, and an antique chandelier set the stage. Often, bending the rules will make for a more interesting and memorable space."

Design by Melissa Palazzo

FRIDA KAHLO/1907.2007

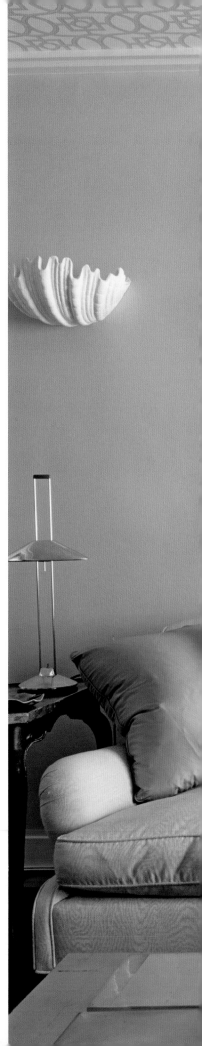

Right: "In an unremarkable New York City apartment building, I set out to create a sophisticated space that showcased my eclectic and modernist aesthetic," says designer James Andrew, who paid homage to his interior designer heroes David Hicks, Billy Baldwin, and Albert Hadley (designers who also gave him many of his featured pieces). "After adding minimalist moldings suitable for a 1950s building to delineate space, I developed a palette of duck-egg blue mixed with chocolate and pops of leaf green and turquoise," says Andrew. By using low-slung furniture, he also created the illusion of height.

Design by James Andrew

Following Pages: "I suppose that I am a maximalist: more is definitely more in my book," says Chassie Post. After living in several apartments with bold color on the walls, Post became obsessed with pattern and wallpapered every square inch of her latest Manhattan loft with birds and butterflies to create a Technicolor aviary. "I think it is really fun to use traditional pattern in a more modern space," says Post. "I love how it's slightly inappropriate!"

Design by Chassie Post

Right: The colors and patterns here simply sizzle up against Miles Redd's signature blue. This room should inspire anyone who has ever considered going bolder—not to mention glossier—on their walls to go for it.

Design by Miles Redd

Following Pages: "I like rooms that resonate with wit and self-assurance and unapologetically say, 'This is who I am—take it or leave it!'" says the ever-fearless designer Mary McDonald. She begged her clients to paint the cream walls gray and, as a result, everything set against them pops with a balanced sense of grandeur.

Design by Mary McDonald

Right: When you feel worried about how all your vintage finds can possibly cohabitate in one room, look at what the Novogratz design duo dynamically demonstrate here: thoughtfully edited placement, with a dash of irreverence (not to mention beautiful, bold artwork), is a decor's best friend.

Design by The Novogratz

Following Pages: In designer Eric Cohler's Manhattan living room, he artfully pairs Gustavian and Louis XVI chairs with a Jonathan Adler tree of life sculpture and an English Regency sofa. Artwork and beloved objects have been hung or displayed intimately rather than showcased to impress. Punctuations of color keep the spirit lively. As a result, the room feels welcoming rather than intimidating. According to Cohler, "It's all in the mix."

Design by Eric Cohler

Right: "For the drawing room in my former apartment on the Upper East Side, it was an exercise in mixing my possessions—antiques and modern pieces—and achieving a balance," says designer Philip Gorrivan. "I decided to paint the walls a deep brown with a bit of aubergine to create a contrast against gold picture frames and light colored furniture. The dark walls added a sense of mystery to an otherwise large square space."

Design by Philip Gorrivan

Following pages:

Left: In a traditional San Francisco 1920s Tudor, designer Geoffrey De Sousa found great bones to play with: "We wanted a masculine, younger, urban vibe," says De Sousa. "Using black-and-white photography alongside George Smith upholstery, and an industrial floor lamp together with a mid-century side table, makes this room current while paying homage to its past."

Design by Geoffrey De Sousa

Right: Fearless can be seamless: case in point, designer Mary McDonald's wall arrangement against the leopard print is what she likes to call "premeditated whimsy." The black and gold frames unify the punch of pattern.

Design by Mary McDonald

Pages 36-37: Whimsical accessories such as a life-size animal statue and bird-patterned lampshades evoke a sense of an *Alice in Wonderland* fantasy in a Brooklyn apartment. Using lush silk drapery and metallic tables and pillows, especially in dark spaces like those often found in New York, helped designer Fawn Galli bring light and glamour to the space.

Design by Fawn Galli

Right: Things don't have to be the same to get along but they should share a similar spirit. Here, treasures that are both exotic and luxurious are casually layered according to height and texture. As a result, the space comes alive and appears receptive to more contributions as the owner's life evolves.

Design by Olivier Gagnere

Following Pages: Simon Doonan and Jonathan Adler are the gold medalists in the "Decorate Fearlessly" Olympics. An open living room in their Shelter Island retreat aims, as Doonan puts it, to be "a blend of Big Sur bohemian and rich Ibiza hippie, two of our favorite adopted personas." By mixing intent with nonchalance, they demonstrate how chic is as much a state of mind as a floor plan.

Design by Jonathan Adler

Pages 42–43: The artwork *Seven Horses* by Jean de Merry anchors the ballroom of this Beaux Arts mansion in Pacific Heights. The grand scale of both the painting and the house inspired designer Geoffrey De Sousa's vision for the nineteenth-century room: "The large space allowed us to play with deep, rich colors, giving it a much more intimate feel," says De Sousa.

Design by Geoffrey De Sousa

When is a mirror more than a mirror? When it's hung in multiples and celebrated not just for its ability to reflect but also for its very frame. This proves the point that you don't need money to start a collection. Just intent and confidence.

Design by Fornasetti

"*T*he Madcap Cottage–designed den is a bit like walking into a British country house in the heart of Brooklyn, with amped-up color and lots of contemporary art," says Jason Oliver Nixon, cofounder of the design firm. "A Venetian gondola–patterned wallpaper from Cole & Sons accents the anchor wall while a beige background in the surrounding fabrics and rug acts as the neutral in the room. Pops of red bring the space to life. A room should be dynamic and never static. High-low, baby, that's how we roll. And you should, too!"

Design by Madcap Cottage

Right: "Mixing antique with modern is fearless when intense color and sleek textures are married," says designer Valorie Hart, who here chose to cover an eighteenth-century daybed in a modern velvet. "Using an overscaled piece of art is super fearless when the color and subject matter is unusual, yet beautiful."

Design by Valorie Hart

Following Pages: Designer Gwynn Griffith shows how a converted factory in Texas can be both grand and intimate by mixing a variety of textures and periods. Her choices—such as placing a modern floor lamp next to a Spanish cabinet—feel deeply her own. "If asked how best to cultivate one's personal style, begin by looking at design books and magazines," advises Griffith. "Don't overthink how the room will come together. It's an organic process and Rome wasn't built in a day. Buy the best pieces you can and that you won't find in a catalogue: you won't be sorry."

Design by Gwynn Griffith

Right: **More is definitely more so don't skimp when you set out to create a visual moment in a room. Why use one floral pattern when two can tango? Why display one glass treasure when several make it all feel so much more special? Sometimes when you abandon your fear, everything flows instead of just "goes."**

Design by Jacqueline Coumans

Following Pages: **"A friend of mine had warned me about 'death by pillows,' but I actually love all the color and variety that they bring to a room," says designer Rodman Primack, who fashioned the ones that decorate the sitting room in his New York apartment from vintage textiles as well as from his own fabric line.**

Design by Rodman Primack

Right: In his own Connecticut sitting room, designer Michael Trapp creates a mood that is both soothing and exotic. Ancient cultures, rich colors, and deep textures work in harmony to create a sense of dimensional poetry that lifts the spirits.

Design by Michael Trapp

Following Pages: Designer Alessandra Branca understands how to walk the tightrope between traditional and unconventional: here she pairs the surprise of citron and coral with very classic fabrics. "I love to punch things up with leopard and coral," says Branca. "The mix of vintage and fine eighteenth-century is a great way to have fun with a room!"

Design by Alessandra Branca

Page 60: Never be afraid to cluster beloved art as high up and as low down as you wish: it creates a delicious intimacy.

Design by Antonello Radi

Page 61: "Wrapping books on a shelf eliminates the visual clutter and includes them as a design element," says Tobi Fairley. "It's also a perfect opportunity to pop in a color that can easily and inexpensively be changed when you need to freshen up!"

Design by Tobi Fairley

"$\mathcal{S}$ince this is a room in my own home, there is a much different process than I might use with a client," says Scot Meacham Wood. "It's a purposefully assembled jumble of mementos, beloved textiles, and an ever-growing collection of artwork, all come to rest in this quiet corner. The small, dark room becomes dramatic and cocoon-like when wrapped in rich colors and layered with memories."

Design by Scot Meacham Wood

Right: Jonathan Adler gives glamour what he calls "arresting twinkle" by layering in metallic accents such as a mirrored coffee table, chrome fire screen, and a silver leather armchair. Combining these twinkles with yummy colors creates a cozy formality.

Design by Jonathan Adler

Following Pages: Both colorful and unconventional, this Los Angeles living room Betsy Burnham designed for clients took a wing chair as its starting point and paired it with a burnt-orange velvet fabric. "We decided to forget the idea of a traditional living room setup and to just do four chairs around a large African drum table," says Burnham. "I kept the wall color quiet and added some colorful ethnic prints, both in the rug and at the windows. It all works for intimate conversations as well as for entertaining."

Design by Betsy Burnham

Right: "I created the look of this room from a strictly limited color palette, which is what makes it remarkably daring for me," says designer Tobi Fairley. "The interplay of different tones and values of green and white, along with the mix of patterns, achieves a final look that is layered but not too visually confusing. It's one of my favorite designs I've ever done."

Design by Tobi Fairley

Following Pages: The various geometric shapes of the furniture, coupled with the playful pattern of the rug, create an offbeat yet elegant environment. Balancing strong colors with neutrals, such as piping a neutral sofa in hot pink and pairing it with softened colors and sheer drapery, creates a space that is alive and engaging, yet not overwhelming.

Design by Fawn Galli

Left: "I loved layering in this eclectic mix of color, patterns, and some images that I've had since high school!" says Sean McNally of his own living room. "It's a very organic process for me. Always buy what feels right and when you put it all together you'll find your story!"

Design by Sean McNally

Following Pages: Color can not only transform a classic space but it can also set the stage for a show-stopping rug and artwork. Make sure all the elements of the room have equal star quality!

Design by Doug Meyer

Pages 76–77: "Decorating isn't about the latest tastes, it's about your taste," says Jane Lilly Warren. "I've found endless inspiration in the things I love, whether it's the eclecticism of Wes Anderson films, the playfulness of Babar, or the classic Palm Beach lifestyle. By incorporating design elements from these places, I'm creating a space that reflects me."

Design by Jane Lilly Warren

*B*y using unconventional design
elements, the fireplace in this 1930s
Georgian-style home is brought into
the twenty-first century. Stainless-steel
tiles on the surround and hearth are
warmed by the deep gray paint shade.
A dark, bold glaze creates a dramatic
luminosity. "Be undaunted in your
approach to mixing styles, periods, and
colors, as these are the very elements
that make a home unique, personal, and
timeless," says its designer Kellie Smith.

Design by Kellie Smith

Right: "Someone once told me: 'Decorating when you have money is easy. Decorating when you don't have any money is a challenge,' says antiques dealer and painter Karina Gentinetta. With her New Orleans home destroyed by Hurricane Katrina, Gentinetta had to pour all her money into rebuilding before considering the decor. "I had to be very savvy and could pick only those items that had meaning to me. Basically, when you lose everything, you really have no more fear. Everything that you acquire or salvage becomes beautiful and treasured. I wanted a place where I could display what I still had in the most open and meaningful way."

Design by Karina Gentinetta

Following Pages: The game room is an old-world luxury, found here in this Edwardian-style home with existing antique checkerboard marble floors. "Don't be afraid to be bold in color and pattern choices," says its designer Stephen Shubel. "It's the best way to keep the games going!"

Design by Stephen Shubel

Left: Sometimes the very display of art becomes an installation in and of itself. Here, gathered beside a daybed, the art also proves that frames need not be uniform in their style and can be hung from floor to ceiling. Such a unique and casual clustering can draw the viewer in even closer than if a singular picture was showcased.

Following Pages: Just because a house's architecture is traditional doesn't mean its decor can't include some sleek pieces. In this room, a leather chair and animal print rug keep the country mix on its toes.

Design by Diego and April Uchitel

*I*n the living room of his Manhattan apartment, William Frawley proves why he is such a deft shoe designer: the sheer beauty of form and material is displayed in a deeply personal way that makes visitors feel like they could pick Frawley out of crowd before they ever met him. The substantial arrangement of the artwork chicly echoes the large windows, their dark twin frames seeming to contain light.

Design by William Frawley

Left: "The full set of bird prints was the first item bought for this house," says its designer, Tom Scheerer. "Framed in bold gold and black bamboo moldings and without mats, they were hung to accentuate the soaring wall height."

Design by Tom Scheerer

Following Pages: "Your home should be your strength in the world," says Marian McEvoy, who not only decorated her Hudson Valley retreat herself, but also did all of its imaginative craftwork, including the upholstery trim, the curtains, and the lampshades. "Decorating is definitely not scary—it should make you happy and delight your friends and family. In the end, decorating is for pleasing people!"

Design by Marian McEvoy

Pages 94–95:

Left: Who says a cottage has to feel entirely cottage-y? Here, the vibe is as much modern as it is country and the dichotomy makes its owner, designer and stylist Jill Sharp Brinson, feel balanced. "My husband's sheep portrait dominates the space and drove me to select visually weighty brown ikat fabric for the traditional chairs," says Jill. "An artist friend cut and installed the twigs and trees in the fireplace box to create a second layer of art and texture."

Right: Sometimes, nostalgia is the best decor muse: "I used crewel fabric on the walls of this sitting room to create a memory I had of a room in my childhood home in Connecticut," says Jill. "The teak shutters and bamboo-carved chairs have followed me from four other homes and play into another memory of my childhood spent in Japan. My favorite dog, Ricky Bobby Brinson, spent many cozy hours by my side in this chair."

Design by Jill Sharp Brinson

𝓜ismatched tables pulled in front of the sofa look somehow grander than one staid long table. "If a room has a theme, then that theme should be you," says its designer, photographer William Waldron. "Don't get trapped by thinking that a room needs certain things, but rather collect things that you love. Then what's to go wrong?"

Design by William Waldron

"*W*e worked to avoid letting any preconceived design ideas about an industrial loft get in the way of using a bold color," says Suysel dePedro Cunningham and Anne Maxwell Foster of the design team Tilton Fenwick. "Hot fuchsia tweed upholstery on funky lounge chairs makes an otherwise color-neutral space pop."

Design by Tilton Fenwick

Right: A cluster of varied framed art and mementos, when displayed with both breadth and depth, has the unified power of a collection. When it comes to displaying your life, more is more as long as it's edited.

Design by Sacha Walckhoff

Following Pages: Stripes give a sense of height and power and delight. Here, the beige and white pattern acts as a kind of neutral with which exotic color and pattern can then be allowed to play.

Design by Suzanne Boyd

GREEKBAAR

BEATON

LIKE A MO

PETER
BUCKLEY

DANISH CHAIRS

SORI YANAGI DESIGN

RIPRODUZIONE DEL DISEGNO ITALIANO
PER L'ARREDAMENTO DOMESTICO

ASSOULINE

ENTRYWAYS

AN ENTRY SHOULD NEVER be merely practical. No matter how muddy your boots nor scattered your keys or mail, this is not a transitory spot simply for depositing and grabbing, but rather it's a place that should reflect who lives inside and how. Whether it's through adding just a few elegant accents as in chez John Cummins on page 111 or using every possible surface to express exuberant creativity as Susan Winberg did on pages 112 and 113, treat your entry with the same consideration as you would your dining room. Even if you never had another visitor, your arrival alone should merit a decor worthy of you.

For Eddie Ross and Jaithan Kochar's Connecticut entry, vivid teal walls and a fiery coral ceiling enliven the greeting of guests with an unexpected dose of drama.

Design by Eddie Ross and Jaithan Kochar

Right: "Nothing defines your home more than your foyer," says designer Jill Sorensen. "The second I come home I want to have my spirits uplifted. A foyer with bold yellow walls, colorful accents, and an animal print is like coming home to exotic sunshine on a rainy day."

Design by Jill Sorensen

Following Pages: While the entry in this Brazilian home is pure beach house, there is also a formality to its whitewashed splendor that allows whatever is put against it—flora, a blue bike, or a statue—to pop like a curated gallery collection.

Design by Sig Bergamin

Right: An entry hall isn't just a place to toss your muck boots and bag. If big enough, it can also showcase art and treasures and relay, at threshold's crossing, the owner's personality. The careful placement of each piece gives this lofty space a formality that still feels welcoming.

Design by John Cummins

Following Pages:

Left: Transitional spaces should always make you want to linger longer. Susan Winberg makes the most out of the entry of her 1836 Greek Revival house by infusing every square inch with whimsy and glamour. Whether stenciling a large ash flower and leaf along the walls in vibrant greens (the property was once called Ash Grove) or painting the front door a miraculous blue, Winberg has created a space that feels like you are walking into someone's imagination.

Right: Any space can become a destination or a chance to let loose and create fantasy within the reality of a house. Use every surface (not to mention height) to full advantage and then keep it grounded by making sure each element is well edited.

Design by Susan Winberg

It would have been so easy to leave this difficult space alone. Instead, the owners created an environment within an environment, smartly infusing it with places to deposit not just treasures, but also themselves. Whether you use it to unwind after a weary day or to energize before a challenging one, by keeping the walls and staircase white, this space allows for clustering that doesn't feel crowded.

"*We* designed this Boston town house for a couple who had just relocated from Manhattan and were about to have their first child—stuffy wasn't going to fly!" says Kristine Irving. "Since it's adjacent to the front entrance, we had the chance to add some edge to otherwise classic architecture. I loved the three-dimensionality of this very flat work of art: it gives a great balance to the gray and black color treatment. This room is really used, so providing it with as much style as we applied to the rest of the home was key. The woodlike planks are actually a woven vinyl floor mat."

Design by Kristine Irving

Right: By placing sturdy English antiques against soft pink walls and adding a sea-horse rug, and add a dash of tropical wallpaper in the entry hall (which Meyer designed), Gene Meyer and Frank de Biasi's Miami home conjures up the Caribbean fantasy houses of Barbados and Mustique.

Design by Gene Meyer and Frank de Biasi

Following Pages: "In one bold statement, we were able to convey the philosophy behind the design of our entire house," says designer Brooke Giannetti. "Surround yourself with natural materials because they mellow and age beautifully over time. And don't be afraid to use overscaled pieces. They are unexpected and add excitement and interest to a space."

Design by Steve and Brooke Giannetti

*B*ookshelves don't have to be bland: make the most of them by giving their surroundings exotic touches, like here on the floor, walls, and ceiling!

Design by Gene Meyer and Frank de Biasi

Right: "Sometimes the most fearless design is to leave a vintage element you love," says Lisa Sherry. "I couldn't resist the original wallpaper in this foyer and knew how amazing it could be to update it with a graphic accent on the wainscoting. A lower than typical entry table makes a unique sculptural expression, while a collection of large-in-scale objects provides height."

Design by Lisa Sherry

Folllowing Pages: What better way to be fearless than with a leopard banquette in the foyer? Juxtaposed against a classic chinoiserie backdrop, this pairing is sophisticated yet playful and makes for a striking welcome!

Design by Melissa Rufty

Right: Picture frames don't need to match, nor must their content be overly precious, to serve as an invaluable portal to an owner's personality from the very moment the door is opened. An entry, of all places, should never take itself too seriously.

Following Pages: Cortney and Robert Novogratz prove that creating an unforgettable entry—here, for two sisters who wanted a bohemian surf retreat in Rockaway Beach—can be as simple as going bold with a paint combination.

Design by The Novogratz

Color can be the ideal architecture to frame and distinguish a room, especially when one space flows into the next. This combination of bold hues proves that a house can hold a lot more than we often give it credit for. Besides, who could ever be sad sitting here?

Design by Liza Bruce and Nicholas Alvis Vega

DINING ROOMS

YOU REALLY SHOULD BE ENTERTAINING in your dining room. I don't just mean in the literal sense of serving delicious food and conversation to seated guests. I mean have FUN with this space! Is there anything worse than sitting in a stuffy, staid dining room? Your guests are captive here, make them grateful they came and serve them things to delight their eyes, not just their taste buds. Take Jamie Drake's exuberant dining room on page 140, featuring a glossy concoction of omnipresent color as delicious as good gossip, or, on pages 148 and 149, Diane Bergeron's fiery dining room, where orange and pink wallpapered walls have the starring role, while the floor and furniture are kept subdued, save for some succulent seat cushions.

A Jean de Merry light fixture looks completely at home hanging above a fairytale-like dining table with tree-trunk bases because it also boasts a playful elegance. Even the eighteenth-century Italian chairs do their part to ensure the room is entertaining as it entertains.

Design by James Aman and John Meeks

Right: "In my dining room, I created this fun, masculine wall of imagined ancestry," says designer Jay Jeffers. "The mix of vintage and contemporary works creates a soulful atmosphere, a feeling of the room having been collected over time. The handsome gray moldings frame the space smartly as well."

Design by Jay Jeffers

Following Pages: "We Madcap Cottage boys were inspired by a visit to the fabled Gritti Palace hotel and wanted to create some of that Venetian-style glamour in our own dining room," says John Loecke, who runs the design firm with his partner Jason Oliver Nixon. "Why not bring your travels home with you? We embellished myriad wallpapers with rhinestones from India to wrap the ceiling. Each dining chair boasts a different fabric and welt. Green is the 'neutral' here."

Design by Madcap Cottage

Left: "Bodacious clients get the most confident rooms," declares designer Jamie Drake, who glossed the ripest papaya color in this New York dining room. Crisp white moldings and Louis XVI–style lacquer frame chairs sporting bright blue cowhide seats and backs with French damask fabric on the outside contrast with a simple, modern ebonized table.

Design by Jamie Drake

Following Pages: "I designed this dining room in the Hamptons to be timelessly decorated with classic beach textures, forms, and colors," says Amanda Nisbet. "By adding the slightly over-scale bright turquoise bead chandelier, I gave the space an unexpected jolt. It lends a high visual impact while not detracting from the pleasant traditional vernacular."

Design by Amanda Nisbet

$\mathcal{M}$iles Redd soothes the unexpected punch of bold colors and stripes with the calming placement of pairs of furniture and accessories of traditional design. The yin-yang dynamic creates a stunning dining room that feels both modern and classical.

Design by Miles Redd

Right: Our client is a connoisseur and avid collector of contemporary and modern art," says Michael Booth of the design firm BAMO. "Starting with one of his favorites, Cady Noland's *Cowboy with Holes, Eating,* we layered wildly diverse pieces to create a livable composition that not only resonates as a collection but also allows each element, including the view, to enjoy distinction. The key to design, like art collecting, is to start with what you love and build from there."

Design by Michael Booth

Following Pages: "I used bold color and pattern to add drama to this traditional dining room," says Diane Bergeron. "The Colonial India– themed toile wallpaper paired with the pink and orange silk curtains create a rich, cozy feeling."

Design by Diane Bergeron

"These rooms are in a town house I designed for a young family in Toronto. We wanted each space to have its own narrative, but also to offer color therapy in a city that is often gray most of the winter," says designer Philip Gorrivan. "At first we were hesitant to hang their art collection on yellow-patterned walls, but the effect was so nice, with both the art and wall-covering balancing each other. I love how the two bold colors—from one room into the next—speak to each other."

Design by Philip Gorrivan

"Dining chairs don't have to match!" says Harry Heissmann, who fashioned this unique dining room on a shoestring budget for a client. "I used nineteenth-century carved American chairs I literally found on the street and then re-caned them. The painting is by an art student. I put the 1900s children's terra-cotta garden stools on the table because I don't like "empty" dining tables. They add color and texture, but most importantly, an unexpected touch of whimsy."

Design by Harry Heissmann

Right: It's important to look at rooms that have a masterful use of color to prove the theory that all hues can cohabitate if just given the chance and the right placement. Here, an unexpected jolt of pink around a door frames not just the entrance but also serves as a backdrop for cool avocado green chairs and a patterned accent wall that stands up to the mix with elegant eccentricity.

Design by Matthew Williamson

Following Pages: "This pool house I designed in the Hamptons was meant to be a bit of a fantasy," says Alessandra Branca. "The blue and white wallpaper was fresh and beachy, but when mixed with the japanned bookshelves and coral, it became an exotic and rich version of a classic."

Design by Alessandra Branca

"Color played a key role in this dining room," says designer Katie Ridder. "Being a room that is inevitably a pass-through between the kitchen and the living room, I wanted it to really sparkle and be as exciting during the day as it is in the evening." With high-gloss walls, a stunning mirrored pendant, fabrics of dramatically different scales, and a contrasting solitary wooden piece, Ridder gives the room distinct dynamism.

Design by Katie Ridder

*G*reat rooms don't need too much when each of their elements are exquisitely designed. Here, the artful lines of chairs echo the art, and the pared-back decor creates a space that inspires both meditation and conversation.

Design by Annabelle Selldorf

Right: "I love to love things that I think other people might not like," says Elizabeth Blitzer of the decor in her mod yet cozy dining room. "I like to look at things that are unexpected and figure out how I would use them differently. I don't want modern or outrageous, but I want unexpected. In a small space, you layer your treasures."

Design by Elizabeth Blitzer

Following Pages: "My client loves intense color, so I let that guide the design process, eventually bringing it to a whole new level with this room," says designer Kara Mann. Drama, however, takes commitment: "The painting process was very involved. First the paint was mixed to match a Larsen fabric that we came across during our design process, then the application required up to five coats with a high-gloss lacquer finish. The resulting paint hue, which I like to describe as a deep, burnt tomato red, set the tone for the rest of the room: fiery and fearless!"

Design by Kara Mann

Right: "Painted floors have been in homes for years, but what really transforms this particular room is the tongue-in-cheek approach," says designer Katie Lydon. "The clients commissioned artist Sun K. Kwak to create a swirl pattern around the central dining space. This touch of whimsy defines the area as a special gathering place, whether as an intimate library or a place to read the morning newspaper."

Design by Katie Lydon

Following Pages:

Left: The banquette, a traditional element of many breakfast rooms, is given a twist with white patent faux croc upholstery and graphic accent pillows. "I'm always striving to find beauty in the mix," says designer Lisa Sherry. "Here, I paired a simple farm table with Lucite seating, glittering mod lighting and a white ram's head."

Design by Lisa Sherry

Right: A kitchen can be functional and fabulous, especially when the dining part is highlighted. By setting the stage with a mostly black-and-white color scheme, the drama is heightened by the whimsical repetition of butterflies and a chandelier straight out of a fairy tale.

Design by Fornasetti

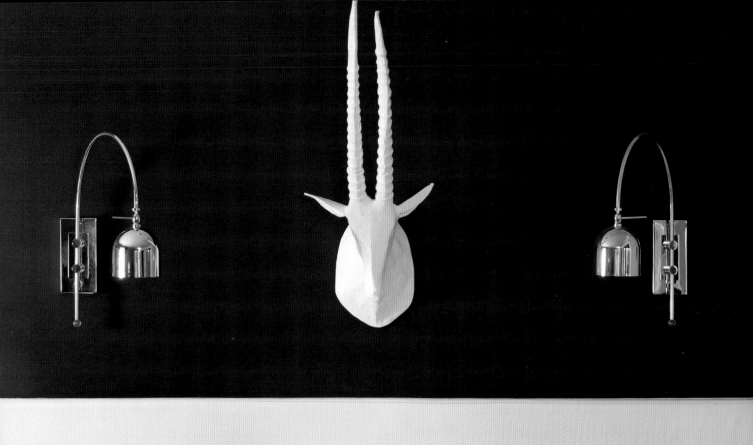

$\mathcal{S}$ometimes being fearless is about accentuating not just your room's architecture but also its location. In their Connecticut dining room, the owners commissioned a custom mural of their surrounding property in the 1800s and then modernized it by adding personal details.

Design by Susan Winberg

"I didn't think twice about covering the walls and ceiling of this dining room in watermelon pink," says designer Julie Massucco Kleiner. "And I was so happy when the painters brushed on the last coat of ceiling gloss. Combined with a traditional brown mahogany table and perked up with white chairs, it is perfectly balanced!"

Design by Julie Massucco Kleiner

KITCHENS

YES YOU COULD GET A LITTLE FEARLESS simply by buying a pink blender or a blue refrigerator and call it a day. But creating a kitchen that will reflect your style and not just your culinary prowess goes a little deeper. Look to add a charismatic light fixture and seats as in this Brooklyn kitchen on page 183, or play with unusual color combinations in the lighting and seating as in Lisa Sherry's kitchen on pages 178 and 179. These well-edited touches only augment the seriousness of the ultimate task at hand: nourishment.

"I had a yellow bedroom as a little girl in the seventies and never used the color again," says designer Denise McGaha. "However, when envisioning a bold show house kitchen, it just called my name. The yellow range started it all. From there, I layered in the graphic fabric backsplash (covered in sheets of glass) and chevron-patterned floor. Yellow makes me smile!"

Design by Denise McGaha

*T*his cozy sitting space within a traditional kitchen is given a stylish twist by employing two modern chairs that don't match yet look perfectly at home alongside a modern table.

Design by Broosk Saib

"I never let the traditional function of a space hold me back," says Lisa Sherry. "My clients craved color and glamour. Cabinets detailed in gold, a lilac chandelier above the work space island, a trio of citron bar stools, and a mosaic-mirrored backsplash all create unexpected touches for a well-orchestrated work space."

Design by Lisa Sherry

*C*olor master Anthony Baratta plays with an unexpected hue in
a kitchen: baby blue. When combined with modern trim and steel
hardware, it morphs from cute to chic. And why not play with pattern on
a kitchen's floor and ceiling? It makes a functional space come alive.

Design by Anthony Baratta

*T*his Brooklyn kitchen proves that modern can still have emotion if you just push the envelope a bit. Here, depth is achieved via the contrast of the matte colors of the chairs and refrigerator alongside the glossy surfaces of the floors and wall.

$\mathcal{E}$ven if it's in the country, Todd Oldham shows how a home can be as much an art installation as a cozy retreat. Unafraid to combine color, art, pattern, and nature, Oldham's explosion of wit and confidence results in a space that reflects a compelling person, rather than a decor.

Design by Todd Oldham

BATHROOMS

A BATHROOM SHOULD BE so much more than a sum of its parts. The downstairs guest bathroom—which impromptu visitors, weekend guests, in-laws and repairmen constantly duck in and out of throughout the year—gets more views than almost any other room of the house besides the kitchen. So why make it ordinary? Nothing makes my heart sink like attending a fabulous dinner in a fabulous house and going to freshen my lipstick in a place that feels generic. If anything, here is a place to go for it! Tuck away that tired tissue box and towel rack. Add instead that wallpaper you've always wanted or a glossy coat of black paint. That crazy shell mirror you craved but feared was overkill in the bedroom . . . not in the bathroom! Scared? Lean on Randolph Martz's design on page 189 as your style crutch. See how far humor, glamour, and color will get you in this not-to-be-forgotten space.

It's rare to find a bathroom that's both feminine and masculine, but London fashion editor Kim Hersov strikes just the right pose, thanks to the juxtaposition of a ladylike light fixture with the dark hues of the tub, a mantel that is original to the mid-nineteenth-century house, and walls painted in Farrow & Ball Mahogany. Feminine final touches like orchids girl it up.

Design by Hubert Zandberg

Right: The bathroom, of all places, is the best room in the house to experiment in getting fearless: the commitment is smaller and the payoff is delightful because who really prefers a serious bathroom? Bring in something intended for another room, like this Roman bust. Turning its importance on its figurative head by placing it in a space far beneath its heritage makes both the bust and the bathroom sing.

Design by Randolph Martz

Following Pages:

Left: "I always say the powder room should be unexpected, if not a diversion, from the rest of the home," remarks designer Melissa Palazzo.

Design by Melissa Palazzo

Right: "I think great pages from books can be as inspiring as high art," says designer Steven Gambrel, who here hand-applied and lacquered the bathroom walls with pages from one of his favorite botanical tomes. "Collections of images that inspire creativity are as important as favorite paintings," he explains.

Design by Steven Gambrel

Right: When it comes to using black and white, it's best to go big or go home, otherwise the bathroom reads as a simply functional space. Here, a stunning collection of black-and-white photography helps envelop the space, along with a folding screen that not only creates privacy, but also more visual drama. An assortment of exotic white coral adds just the right reminder that somewhere outside this glamorous cocoon an ocean awaits.

Design by Hubert Zandberg

Following Pages:

Left: An oversize floral pattern completely transforms a bathroom wall. With the gold color dressing it up and the picture accents bringing the glamour down a notch, a perfect balance between dressy and day-to-day is achieved. A bathroom is an ideal place to try a bold wallpaper pattern you've always dreamed of but never dared.

Design by Matthew Williamson

Right: "This lowly woodshed was reborn as the chicest bathroom in my house," says designer Darren Henault. "Keeping the elements in the room basic, yet funky, referenced its origins, although the dirt floor had to go. Humble can be glorious."

Design by Darren Henault

BEDROOMS

I THINK PEOPLE PLAY IT TOO SAFE in the bedroom. So often we talk about having a space that's "serene" and "restful." But in striving for comfort, we can end up with white caves that feel empty, where a bed and dresser make an appearance out of obligation. If you think about it, a bedroom void of personality is often the hardest to fall asleep in because it doesn't feel like anyone lives there. The more care you take in its rendering, the better care it will ultimately give you. So don't be afraid here. Use rich color and whimsy with abandon as a way to cocoon, as elegantly exemplified in Fabrizio Rollo's bedroom in Brazil, opposite, or pare down and let the architecture and texture of the space do the talking as in Jill Sharp Brinson and Rob Brinson's loftlike bedroom in Atlanta on page 218. Every bedroom in this chapter feels like stepping into its owner's dreams as much as it seeks to provide sweet ones. Wherever the space, create an edited environment which soothes and invigorates. After all, you wake up here, too.

A wallpapered wall provides depth and an ideal backdrop upon which to layer more color, form, and pattern. More isn't just more here: it's downright harmonious when paired with confidence.

Design by Fabrizio Rollo

$\mathcal{K}$ids know how to be fearless from the
get-go because not even the brightest of
colors can trump their inner expressions.
For parents cautious about painting
an entire room pink, an accent wall is
a great way to go. The bed/sofa here is
particularly fabulous (not to mention
resourceful)—an uber-chic command
central for juicy gossip sessions and
much-deserved sleep.

Design by Jonathan Adler

Right: In making a bedroom for her ninety-year-old mother, the renowned designer Betty Sherrill, Ann Pyne—herself an acclaimed interior designer—strove to create a bed glamorous enough for her spunky and headstrong "client." The Zoffany floral wallcovering was the visual start and from there dictated the show-stopping satin fabric that both cocoons and, as Pyne puts it, "gussies up" the four-poster bed. "It's with the details that decorating fearlessly takes place," says Pyne.

Design by Ann Pyne

Following Pages:

Left: If you love a color combination, don't contain it, let it play itself evenly out throughout a room, right down to the window frame.

Design by Ilaria Miani

Right: Draping such strong colors on a bedroom's walls and linens feels surprisingly serene instead of silly. By keeping the walls bare and letting the hues do the talking, the space feels almost monastic.

Design by Andrea Gobbi

"*E*ven though I designed this room for a teen girl, I would move right in!" says designer Rodman Primack. "It all started with the amazing vinyl mural by the Brazilian artist collective Assume Vivid Astro Focus. There was so much going on after that, that I just kept throwing more at it: from my favorite David Hicks pattern upholstered behind the bed, to the hot pink rug with real copper stripes. It is a riot of color and periods, but it is youthful without being childish."

Design by Rodman Primack

A bedroom can get its style simply from the kick of the right accessories. A row of prints acts as an unofficial headboard to a bed popped by the wink of a Warhol-style banana pillow and a ruby-red rug below. The arc of a lamp feels both maternal and modern.

Design by Naeem Khan

Right: "Bright color in a bedroom is fearless," says Valorie Hart. "You can use a fabric-covered accent wall as an alternative to paint. The exhilarating emerald green I chose here is reinforced by upholstering the headboard and bench in an overscaled bright green toile."

Design by Valorie Hart

Following Pages: "Instead of sticking to one strong color or pattern in this garden-inspired bedroom, I mixed several of both to create a bright and cheerful space," says designer Nick Olsen. "The key is scale and adjacency: the bold floral sofa meets a crisp white bed; the pink and green striped wall ends in white trim and a neutral sisal carpet. Shocking pink, bottle green, and turquoise can live in harmony if given some relief!"

Design by Nick Olsen

For his Miami bedroom, Doug Meyer covered the walls floor to ceiling with blue collage. "It took almost six months to collect the right images and colors from books and magazines," says Meyer. "In the end it's very tranquil, like waking up in an aquarium."

Design by Doug Meyer

Right: Blue feels serene and stylish when paired with lots of white and hints of gold. Accessories that are hung according to whim rather than rules keep the spirit exotic instead of too serious.

Design by Fabrizio Rollo

Following Pages: Accentuate the quirkiness of a room's architecture by going all out in the wallpaper department, eaves and all. And then why not continue the spirit in a slightly different take on the bed and chair upholstery? This master bedroom proves how far you can go, especially when such a fabulous floral pattern is used.

Design by Jacqueline Coumans

Left: "Our esoteric Atlanta bedroom, located in a larger-than-life space, is the dream that I always imagined," says stylist and designer Jill Sharp Brinson of the 10,000-square-foot loft she shares with her husband, photographer Rob Brinson. "Waking up in the natural light of this room surrounded by a sea of nothing is a visual and visceral experience. I ruthlessly edited the room so the vibe is highly personal and a reflection of us."

Design by Jill Sharp Brinson

Following Pages:

Left: There's no better place to play with scale and pattern than a child's room. Children aren't afraid of mixing color and scale so why should you be?

Design by Melissa Palazzo

Right: "I encourage people to experiment with scale, " says designer Fawn Galli. "Playing with the scale of figurative wallpaper envelops you and brings you into the space. The large lily pads give a dreamy feeling, and the white sheer drapes are ethereal. Using mirrors enhances the all-encompassing dimensionality of the room."

Design by Fawn Galli

"I love waking up every morning in an enchanted forest," says designer Alex Papachristidis of his bedroom. "The importance of nature in a room cannot be overstated." And while the leafy patterned wall dominates the room, there's an even layering of both texture and color overall. Note how he elegantly extends the whimsical headboard by having fun with unique wall art.

Design by Alex Papachristidis

The bed doesn't have to have all the fun. Why not turn the walls into an exotic cocoon by covering them with an oversize colorful pattern that delights rather than overwhelms? The space is grounded by distinct pops of coral paired with a textured gold poster bed that harmonizes with the tropical theme.

Design by Kate McIntyre and Brad Huntzinger

"*I* took the traditional, classic concept of using toile throughout a room, but selected one with unusually modern colors," says Alex Papachristidis. By mixing in a geometric-patterned carpet with organic walls and bold red satin, the effect is both modern and classic.

Design by Alex Papachristidis

Inspired by an antique sari found in San Miguel de Allende, Mexico, designer Gwynn Griffith commissioned her oldest son to paint the mural in her San Antonio, Texas, bedroom; it transports and envelops the room with its rich colors and exotic depictions. The rest of the bedroom feels equally exotic but never at the expense of comfort.

Design by Gwynn Griffith

Right: Why go for just a headboard when an entire screen can provide even more architectural detail to your bedroom? Framing it against a backdrop of robin's egg blue gives further distinction.

Following Pages:

Left: Whether you live in Minnesota or Miami, the visual landscapes throughout your house can either reflect your actual location or where you dream to live. When it's the latter, even the most ordinary nook can feel exotic.

Design by Hubert Zandberg

Right: "I love when wall and furniture begin to melt into one another," says Doug Meyer of this Manhattan guest room he designed where green dominates. The custom headboard of Plexiglas and painted wood boasts fives shades of green. "The plush rug and rich fabrics on the bed and windows create a cocoon-like safe environment," adds Meyer.

Design by Doug Meyer

Right: Why not treat the fireplace as a design opportunity? Here in his black and white bedroom, designer Matthew Williamson has wrapped his in a custom commissioned floral pattern and created a graphic formality softened by whimsy.

Design by Matthew Williamson

Following Pages:

Left: "I adore stripes!" says designer Melissa Warner Rothblum. "Painting them horizontally on your walls is a great way to add personality and interest to any space. In this little boy's room, pairing the bold navy and ivory stripes with a tangerine upholstered headboard and Lucite nesting tables created a playful and fresh look."

Design by Melissa Warner Rothblum

Right: Color is a social entity and it plays best when it plays with others," says Leslie DeVito. "When making over my daughter's bedroom for her thirteenth birthday, rather than allow one color to dominate, we chose a quartet of complementary colors and a joyful energy resulted from their equal interplay."

Design by Lesli DeVito

$\mathcal{T}$hink of how different this bedroom would look without the impact of that chandelier. If your space lacks pizzazz, invest in one razzle-dazzle lighting fixture. Troll flea markets and Ebay. It doesn't even have to work, its visual impact will bring in that much needed oomph to the space, especially one with a high ceiling. Your bedside lamps can take care of the light. Your chandelier just needs to look glamorous.

Design by Elizabeth Blitzer

Right: Using a graphic black-and-white wallpaper and a contemporary ikat fabric as a launching point for this bedroom, Kriste Michelini then began to fearlessly mix bold patterns and build the palette by incorporating vibrant colors such as lavender, hot pink, green, and black. The fur pillow and zebra rug add texture while the chandelier lends glamour.

Design by Kriste Michelini

Following Pages: British designer Ashley Hicks brilliantly demonstrates how personal change can become a design impetus: "When my wife and I separated, I painted the walls of the bedroom with a random block-work design in madder reds, of which she would not have approved. The bedside tables are my crescent design with gilded legs, and the headboard is covered in David Hicks Topkapi Tulip velvet—its colors very much like those of the 1750s chair in the photograph above, which I took at Stupinigi, the beautiful Baroque hunting lodge near Turin."

Design by Ashley Hicks

$\mathcal{U}$sing formal accessories that are normally reserved for a living room gives a weighty uptick to a bedroom's style. Just make sure your bed is dressed up for the occasion too.

Design by Roland Nivelais

DESIGNER CREDITS

247

Andrea Gobbi
Bedrooms, p. 203
www.andreagobbi.com

Philip Gorrivan
Living Rooms, p. 33; Dining
Rooms, p.151
www.philipgorrivan.com

Gwynn Griffith
Living Room, pp. 50-51;
Bedrooms, p. 228
www.gwynngriffith.com

Valorie Hart
Living Room, p. 49; Bedrooms,
p. 209
www.valoriehart.com

Harry Heissmann, Inc
Dining Rooms, p. 153
www.harryheissmanninc.com

Darren Henault
Bathroom, p. 195
www.darrenhenault.com

Ashley Hicks
Bedrooms, pp. 242-243
www.ashleyhicks.com

Kristine Irving, Koo de Kir
Entryways, p. 117
www.koodekir.com

Jay Jeffers
Dining Rooms, p. 137
www.jeffersdesigngroup.com

Naeem Khan
Bedrooms, pp. 206-207
www.naeemkhan.com

Julie Massucco Kleiner
Dining Rooms, p. 173
www.massuccowarnermiller.com

Katie Lydon
Dining Rooms, p. 167
www.katielydoninteriors.com

Madcap Cottage
Living Room, p. 47; Dining Room,
pp. 138-139; Bedroom, front cover
www.madcapcottage.com

Kara Mann
Dining Rooms, pp. 164-164
www.karamann.com

Mary McDonald
Living Rooms, pp. 26-27, p. 35
www.marymcdonaldinc.com

Marian McEvoy
Living Rooms, pp. 92-93

Denise McGaha Interiors
Kitchens, p. 174
www.denisemcgaha.com

Kate McIntyre & Brad
Huntzinger
Bedrooms, p. 225
www.olystudio.com

Sean McNally
Living Room, p. 72
seanmcon45@gmail.com

Scot Meacham Wood Design
Living Room, p. 63
www.smwdesign.com

Doug Meyer
Living Rooms, pp. 74-74;
Bedroom, p. 213, p. 233
www.dougandgenemeyer.com

Gene Meyer and
Frank de Biasi
Entryways, p. 119; Entryway, p. 123
www.dougandgenemeyer.com

Ilaria Miani
Bedrooms, p. 202
www.ilariamiani.com

Kriste Michelini
Bedrooms, p. 241
www.kristemichelini.com

Amanda Nisbet Design
Dining Rooms, pp. 142-143
www.amandanisbetdesign.com

Roland Nivelais
Bedrooms, p. 245
www.rolandnivelais.com

The Novogratz
Living Room, p. 29; Entryways,
pp. 130-131
www.thenovogratz.com

Todd Oldham
Kitchens, p. 185
www.toddoldham.com

Nick Olsen
Bedrooms, pp. 210-211
www.nickolsenstyle.com

Melissa Palazzo of
Pal + Smith
Living Rooms, pp. 18-19;
Bathrooms, p. 190; Bedrooms,
p. 220
www.palandsmith.com

Alex Papachristidis
Living Rooms, pp. 12-13;
Bedrooms, p. 223; Bedrooms,
p. 226
www.alexpapachristidis.com

Chassie Post
Living Rooms, pp. 22-23
Rodman Primack
Living Room, pp. 54-55;
Bedrooms, p. 204
www.chassiepost.com

Ann Pyne
Bedrooms, p. 201
www.mcmilleninc.com

Antonello Radi
Living Rooms, p. 60
www.antonelloradi.com

Miles Redd
Living Room, p. 25; Dining
Rooms, p.145
www.milesredd.com

Katie Ridder
Dining Rooms, p. 158
www.katieridder.com

Fabrizio Rollo
Bedrooms, p. 197, p. 215
www.fabriziorollo.com

Eddie Ross and Jaithan
Kochar
Entryways, p. 104
www.eddieross.com

Melissa Warner Rothblum
of Massucco Warner Miller
Interior Design© 2013
Living Rooms, pp. 16-17;
Bedrooms, p. 236
www.massuccowarnermiller.com

Melissa Rufty
Entryways, pp. 126-127
www.mmrinteriors.com

Broosk Saib
Kitchens, p. 177
www.broosk.com

Tom Scheerer
Living Rooms, p. 90
www.tomscheerer.com

Annabelle Selldorf
Dining Rooms, pp. 160-161
www.selldorf.com

Lisa Sherry,
Lisa Sherry Interieurs
Living Rooms, p. 15; Entry Ways,
p. 125; Dining Rooms, p. 167;
Kitchens, pp. 178-179
www.lisasherryinterieurs.com

Stephen Shubel
Living Room, pp. 82-83
www.stephenshubel.com

Kellie Smith
Living Room, p. 79
www.kelliesmithdesignstudio.com

Jill Sorensen
Entryways, p. 107
www.marmaladeinteriors.com

Michael Trapp
Living Room, p. 57
www.michaeltrapp.com

Diego and April Uchitel
Living Rooms, pp. 86-87
www.diegouchitel.com

Sacha Walckhoff -
Creative Director for
Christian Lacroix
Living Rooms, p. 101

William Waldron
Living Rooms, p. 97
www.williamwaldron.com

Jane Lilly Warren
Living Room, pp. 76-77

Matthew Williamson
Dining Rooms, p. 155; Bathrooms,
p. 194; Bedrooms, p. 235
www.matthewwilliamson.com

Susan Winberg, Zoma
Design
Entryway, pp. 112-113; Dining
Room, p. 171
slw4083@aol.com

Hubert Zandberg
Bathrooms, p. 186; Bathrooms,
p.193; Bedrooms, p. 232
www.hzinteriors.com

PHOTOGRAPHY CREDITS

Living Rooms

Entryways

Dining Rooms

Kitchens

Bathrooms

Bedrooms

ACKNOWLEDGMENTS

My profuse thanks and admiration for all the designers featured here. They continue to inspire me with their fearless embrace, not just of design, but of life.

For my amazing Rizzoli editor, Ellen Nidy, who always gets it, even before I get it. And for Rizzoli's Charles Miers who, thankfully, gets us both.

Many thanks to all the incredible photographers who captured these fearless rooms with equal parts respect and glamour and shared them with me.

And thanks to Jason Snyder, Doug Turshen and David Huang for arranging the images with the care of surgeons and the eye of painters.

Front cover: "We pushed petals aplenty in our guest bedroom," says Jason Oliver Nixon. "The room truly blooms with pattern and color, and the mix of various Thibaut wallpapers with stunning fabrics is heady and delicious. We used a vibrant yellow hue from Farrow & Ball to paint the moldings, and many of the furnishings are vintage. Have fun with pattern and color! Pick one tone and use it throughout a room to create a consistent voice and storyline. Just remember: Good design need not be expensive, but it should always be expressive."

Design by Madcap Cottage

Page 2: Jonathan Adler has mastered the art of being cheeky and chic. Here delicious pops of orange and turquoise lighten the luxurious load of the deep wood paneling in a New York townhouse. The flirty crystal sailboat is the room's ultimate jewelry.

Design by Jonathan Adler

First published in the United States of America in 2014 by
Rizzoli International Publications, Inc.
300 Park Avenue South, New York, NY 10010
www.rizzoliusa.com

Book design by Jason Snyder

Editor: Ellen Nidy

Design Coordinator: Kayleigh Jankowski

2014 2015 2016 2017 2018 / 10 9 8 7 6 5 4 3 2 1

ISBN-13: 978-0-8478-4233-9

Library of Congress Control Number: 2013956497

Printed and bound in China

Distributed to the U.S. trade by Random House